D0368864

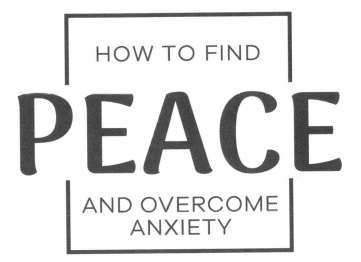

HOW TO FIND

PEACE

AND OVERCOME
ANXIETY

igloobooks

igloobooks

Written by Gemma Barder
Designed by Simon Parker
Edited by Natalie Graham

Copyright © 2020 Igloo Books Ltd

Published in 2020
First published in the UK by Igloo Books Ltd
An imprint of Igloo Books Ltd
Cottage Farm, NN6 0BJ, UK
Owned by Bonnier Books
Sveavägen 56, Stockholm, Sweden

Manufactured in China. 1120 001
10 9 8 7 6 5 4 3 2 1

Library of Congress Cataloging-in-Publication
Data is available upon request.

ISBN 978-1-83903-782-5
IglooBooks.com
bonnierbooks.co.uk

INTRODUCTION

When anxiety builds, it can affect our lives in many different ways. It can lead to lack of concentration, periods of depression, and long-term health issues. However, there are lots of techniques, advice, and tips that can help when you feel your anxiety growing.

This book is full of meditations, breathing exercises, writing activities, and inspiring quotes for you to flip through whenever you feel the need. Keep it on your desk, by your bed, or on the kitchen counter – ready to find an exercise that is just right for you.

Although the activities in this book can help to calm your anxiety, always consult with a doctor if you feel your anxiety is too much to handle.

WORRYING IS LIKE RIDING
A ROCKING HORSE.
IT WON'T GET
YOU ANYWHERE.

YOUR PERFECT SPACE

When we feel anxious, we crave somewhere familiar where we can completely be ourselves. Use the list below to plan what your ideal space would contain. Would you want your favorite weighted blanket, a candle that always makes you feel relaxed, or certain snacks and drinks?

USE THIS LIST THE NEXT TIME YOU NEED A SAFE SPACE TO RELAX.

Which candle or diffuser would you have?

Blankets and pillows?

Snacks and drinks?

TV show, movie, or book?

Are people allowed? If so, who? Or is this just your space?

The Basics of Meditation

ALL MEDITATIONS FOLLOW A PATTERN
OF BREATHING AND THE ABILITY TO
CONNECT WITH YOUR BREATH.
IF YOU ARE NEW TO MEDITATION
OR SHORT ON TIME, FOLLOW
THESE SIMPLE STEPS FOR A BASIC
MEDITATION EXERCISE.

1. Sit or lie down in a comfortable position.

2. Take a deep breath in through your nose and out through your mouth.

3. Continue to breathe and listen to your breath.

4. Feel where your body makes contact with the ground, the chair, or the bed you are on.

5. Feel where your body makes contact with itself. Are your ankles crossed? Are your hands on your lap? Feel the weight and the warmth of them.

6. Continue to listen to your breath.

7. If a thought comes into your head that isn't about your breath or your body, calmly acknowledge it and let it drift out of your mind.

8. Once you feel you have let all your thoughts go, start to 'wake up.' Circle your wrists, circle your ankles, and roll your shoulders.

9. Slowly open your eyes.

Tip: You may need a few moments or a glass of water before you can stand up and continue your day.

BREATHING EXERCISES

This simple technique is perfect if you are out of the house and feel you need a moment of calm.

This technique will help to calm your nerves and give your mind something else to focus on. It is perfect if you are feeling anxious at work or in a public space as it can be completed quickly.

1. Find a quiet place. This could be in your car, or even the bathroom if you are at work or have people at home.

2. Close your eyes.

3. Breathe in slowly through your nose as you count to 5, letting your stomach inflate.

4. Breathe out slowly through your mouth as you count down from 5, blowing your anxiety away.

5. Repeat at least three times. Do more if you can or if you feel you need to.

NEGATIVE EMOTIONS

This activity will help you to come to terms with a moment in your life that you might think back on with negativity. Take a moment to think about what that moment was, then fill out the answers to these questions:

What happened to make this a negative moment for you?

If you think you were at fault, why do you think you did what you did?

If you think someone else was at fault, why do you think they did what they did?

If you could give advice to the person you were when this moment happened, what would you say?

List three things that could happen to make you feel better about this situation.

1.

2.

3.

FOUR · SEVEN · EIGHT

An expanded version of the 1 to 5 technique, this exercise will calm your mind as you focus on your breath.

1. Find a quiet spot and close your eyes.

2. Take a deep breath in through your nose for 4 seconds, imagining you are filling your stomach with air.

3. Hold your breath for 7 seconds.

4. Now release all the air in your stomach slowly for 8 seconds.

5. Repeat the exercise at least twice, or more if you have time.

Tip: If you cannot hold your breath for 7 seconds, don't worry. You may have taken in too much air. On your second go, try breathing in more slowly as you count to 4.

TENSE & relax

This meditation will connect you with your body and release the tension you may not even realize you are holding on to.

1. Lie on a mat on the floor, or on a bed if it is more comfortable.

2. Let your feet flop to the side and turn your palms upwards.

3. Close your eyes and take a few deep breaths in through your nose and out through your mouth.

4. Starting at your feet, acknowledge any tension you feel and let it go.

5. Work your way up through your legs, hips, stomach, arms, hands, shoulders, and neck. At each point, think about any tension or stress you are holding on to and let it go.

6. As you reach your face, imagine the space between your eyes spreading and relaxing. Let any tension in your head disappear through the top of your head.

7. After a pause, begin to wiggle your fingers and toes.

8. Roll on to your side and bring yourself up into a sitting position.

Tip: This meditation is great at the end of the day, and will help you to relax before bedtime.

LETTER TO YOURSELF

Imagine that you are not you.
Imagine that you are a friend, parent,
or a sibling of yours. What would you
say to someone who feels the way you
do when you are low, sad, or upset?
Sometimes it's hard to be as nice
to yourself as you are to others!

USE THIS SPACE TO WRITE A LETTER TO YOURSELF:

GIVE YOURSELF PERMISSION TO MAKE MISTAKES.

TRIGGER & RELEASE

There are certain things that trigger anxiety in us. It could be seeing a person, remembering a moment, or even hearing a song. List five of your triggers on a piece of paper, then write down a reason to be grateful for that trigger underneath.

For example:

Trigger: Seeing that person who used to be a friend.

Release: Letting go of the anger and sadness you feel towards them. Not letting it affect your day. Wish them well if you can.

YOU CANNOT POUR
FROM AN EMPTY JUG.
TAKE TIME TO FILL
YOURS UP.

ANXIETY DOES NOT TAKE
AWAY TOMORROW'S
TROUBLES, IT TAKES
AWAY TODAY'S JOY.

Walking
Meditation

This meditation brings you out of your thoughts and focuses your mind on action.

1. Find a spot where you can walk 10-15 steps. It could be out in your backyard, or inside if you prefer. You may find that outside in nature works best.

2. Start by walking 10-15 steps, pausing, turning, and walking 10-15 steps back.

3. As you walk, focus on each step. Notice how your foot lifts off the ground and swings forward. Afterwards, notice how your foot is placed back on the floor.

4. Walk slowly and deliberately. Notice how your body reacts to each step.

5. If you feel other thoughts creeping into your mind, dismiss them happily and focus back on your steps

6. When you have walked – concentrating on your steps for at least four turns – think about stopping. Be aware that it may take you a few cycles to get to this place.

Tip: Walking meditation is a form of mindfulness that helps you to connect to the here and now. It's a great way to calm a busy mind.

GRATITUDE JOURNAL

Think back over the past week. No matter how stressful it might have been, try to think of something you were grateful for each day. It could be as simple as having enough gasoline to get you to work! Start on the day of the week it is today and work backwards.

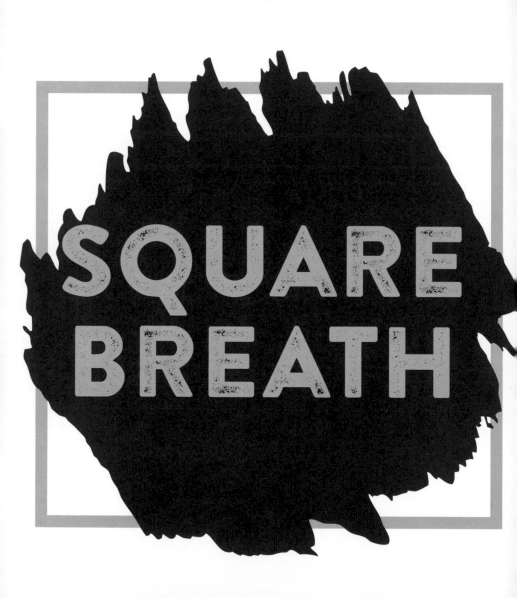

Holding your breath sends a signal to your brain and can help release endorphins.

1. Draw a square on a piece of paper. If you are out and about, imagine a square on your leg or any flat surface.

2. Place your finger in the top left-hand corner of the box.

3. Breathe in through your nose, slowly counting to 4 as your finger moves across to the top right-hand corner.

4. Hold your breath for a count of 4 as your finger moves down to the bottom right-hand corner of your square.

5. Exhale through your mouth, counting slowly to 4 as your finger slides to the bottom left-hand corner.

6. Hold your breath for a count of 4 as your finger moves back to the top left-hand corner of your square.

7. Repeat as many times as you need.

Tip: Match the speed of your finger to your breath. Don't try to go too quickly or too slowly.

Meditation Notes

Choose one of the
meditations in this book.
Once you have finished it,
answer the questions below.

What type of meditation did you do?

....

....

....

Why did you feel the urge to meditate today?

....

....

....

How did you feel before you started the meditation?

....

....

....

How did you feel after the meditation?

....

....

....

Did anything surprise you about what you visualized or how you felt?

....

....

....

What was the best thing about this meditation?

....

....

....

Gather the crumbs of happiness to make a loaf of contentment.

BE AS KIND TO
YOURSELF AS YOU
ARE TO THE PEOPLE
YOU LOVE MOST IN
THE WORLD.

Beach and boat visualization

Read this visualization story before you begin your meditation. It will work like a guided meditation.

1. Sit in a comfortable position and read the story below. Have it clearly in your mind before you begin:

You are standing on a beach. It can be any beach, real or imagined, at any time of day, in any weather. Walk along the beach, watching your feet make footprints. Register what your feet look like. Do they have shoes on? Are you barefoot?

On the horizon is a boat that comes to shore. Who is in the boat? Is it empty?

As you climb into the boat, imagine your anxiety is left behind on the shore. If it helps, give your anxiety a physical quality. It could be a box with your worries inside, or something more descriptive.

As you breathe, imagine the boat taking you out to the ocean, leaving your anxiety on the shore. Soon there is only the Ocean, the boat, and whoever is in the boat with you. Pause in the boat for a few breaths.

Finally, imagine the boat gently coming back to the beach, and this time, whatever represented your anxiety is gone.

2. Now, close your eyes and take a deep breath in through your nose and out through your mouth.

3. Listen to your breath and feel where your body makes contact with the ground, the chair, or the bed you are on.

4. Start to tell the story to yourself in your mind. Try not to rush through the stages. Remember: Beach, boat, leave your anxiety behind on the shore, ocean, return.

5. Slowly open your eyes.

HAPPY TIMES

Stress and anxiety can build like a tidal wave.
It can often be hard to see the good for all the bad that
can cloud our minds. This exercise is a great way of
remembering times that were joyous and filled with light.

Write down a happy time in your life, then list the
way it made you feel.

For example:

Happy time: Day trip to Malibu, swimming in the ocean.
Feelings: Loved. Healthy. Relaxed. Secure. Grateful.
Proud. Happy. Full.

Happy time:
Feelings:

Happy time:
Feelings:

Happy time:
Feelings:

Happy time:
Feelings:

ELEVATOR BREATH

Control your inhaling breath for this de-stressing technique.

1. This breath works better if you are in a standing position. Stand with your feet hip-width apart and close your eyes.

2. Image that your breath begins at your feet and slowly start to inhale ⅓ of your breath up to your thighs. Pause.

3. Now continue to inhale up to your shoulders for another ⅓. Pause.

4. Finish your inhale by imagining it is reaching the top of your head.

5. Now slowly blow out your breath, along with any anxiety and tension you may be feeling.

Tip: It can be tricky to split your inhaling breath into three, but a little practice makes this exercise worth the effort!

POSITIVITY ACTIVITY

We tend to remember negative situations more clearly than positive ones. The following questions are designed to trigger those memories you may have buried.

Write down a time you felt proud:

....

....

....

Write down a time you laughed until your stomach hurt:

....

....

----

write down a time you felt loved:

....

....

....

....

write down a time you felt
completely relaxed:

....

....

....

....

write down a time you achieved something
you thought you might not:

....

....

....

....

HOW TO SAY 'NO'

Saying no to someone can be a trigger for anxiety. Will the person you said no to still like you? Will they ask you again? Will that offer of work ever come to you again if you turn it down this time?

Saying no is brave. It is also very difficult for anxiety sufferers.

THINK ABOUT A TIME WHEN YOU SAID YES, WHEN YOU REALLY WANTED TO SAY NO. IT COULD HAVE BEEN TO A FRIEND, A BOSS, OR A FAMILY MEMBER. WRITE DOWN HOW YOU THINK THEY WOULD HAVE REACTED. IF YOU HAD SAID NO, WOULD IT HAVE BEEN AS BAD AS YOU THOUGHT?

I SAID YES WHEN I WANTED TO SAY NO WHEN...

THEIR REACTION WOULD PROBABLY HAVE BEEN...

THE
NOSTRIL
BREATH

This breath may feel a little strange at first, but it helps to activate the calming sections of your brain.

1. Sit somewhere quiet and in a comfortable position.

2. Take your thumb and ring finger and place them on either side of your nose.

3. Press your thumb against your right nostril and take a breath in through your left nostril for a count of 3.

4. Release your thumb and press your ring finger against your left nostril. Breathe slowly for a count of 3 out of your right nostril.

5. Leave your fingers where they are and take a deep breath in through your right nostril.

6. Repeat for as many times as needed.

Tip: If you feel a little silly doing this exercise, make sure you are somewhere you won't worry about being disturbed.

All you need is *love!*

Sometimes, listing the things we love can fill up our own hearts, too. Write down your answers and then think about why you love them.

Name three people
you love:

1.
2.
3.

Name three of your
favorite places to
visit:

1.
2.
3.

Name three of your
favorite meals:

1.
2.
3.

Name three of your
favorite books:

1.
2.
3.

Name three of your
favorite movies or TV
shows:

1.
2.
3.

Name three of your
favorite hobbies:

1.
2.
3.

Resistance
Breathing

CONTROLLING THE BREATH THAT COMES OUT OF YOUR MOUTH CAN HELP TO TAKE YOUR MIND AWAY FROM YOUR ANXIETY TRIGGERS.

1. Sit in a comfortable position. Have a glass of water nearby in case you feel lightheaded. Make sure you are somewhere where you won't be disturbed for the next 20 minutes or so.

2. Close your eyes.

3. Take a breath in through your nose for 4 counts.

4. As you breathe out through your mouth, clench your teeth and place the tip of your tongue behind your front teeth.

5. It should take a while to empty your breath, and your brain should focus only on the technique.

6. Repeat three times.

TIP: IF YOU START TO FEEL DIZZY, STOP THE TECHNIQUE AND TAKE THREE DEEP BREATHS IN AND OUT AS YOU WOULD NORMALLY BREATHE.

IF YOU WANT TO FLY,
GET RID OF ANYTHING THAT
WEIGHS YOU DOWN.

THE WORRY LIST

Worries can buzz around our minds like flies. They steal focus from what is truly important and can drain our energy. Finding something practical to do about your worries is often a great way of banishing them.

Use the space below to list each of the worries you have now, and how you can help them fly away.

For example:
I am worried about... my parents coping in their house as they get older. So, I will... talk to them about it the next time I am there/ look into alarm systems/ research the cost of cleaning staff.

I am worried about:

....

....

....

....

Every day may not be good, but there is good in every day.

AWARENESS BREATHING

This exercise will help to take your mind away from whatever is triggering your anxiety and bring it back to your body.

1. Sit comfortably somewhere. This could be on a chair or cross-legged on the floor.

2. Close your eyes and take a deep breath in through your nose for a count of 3.

3. Exhale through your mouth for a count of 3.

4. On your next inhalation, notice how your chest expands, how your shoulders/shoulder blades move, and how your head feels. Pause.

5. On your exhalation, notice what happens to your torso, your arms, and your chest.

6. With each breath, try to focus on another part of your body that changes as you breathe in and out.

7. Repeat the breath at least four times. When you have finished, stand up and gently shake your limbs.

Tip: Focusing the mind on your body takes the focus away from your triggers. Try really hard to stay focused on your body throughout this exercise.

Muscle Relaxation

This meditation is perfect for helping with nerves. It makes your body feel loose by eliminating any built-up tension.

1. This exercise works best if you are lying down on a mat on the floor. If you find this uncomfortable, you can lie on a bed.

2. Close your eyes and take a deep breath in through your nose and out through your mouth.

3. Listen to your breath and feel where your body makes contact with the ground, the chair, or the bed you are on.

4. Starting at your feet, tense all the muscles for the length of one inhalation.

5. As you exhale, let all the tension go.

6. Continue up your body, tensing each muscle as you inhale, and releasing with the exhale.

7. When you reach your head, scrunch up your face as you inhale, and release as you exhale.

8. Take a few deep breaths at the end of your meditation to finish.

Tip: As you exhale and release, imagine you are blowing the muscle tension away.

Comfort Zone

In all our lives, we have things we enjoy doing, things we don't mind, and things we absolutely hate! We feel differently depending on what we are doing at the time. For example, you may love going for coffee with your sister but feel completely differently going for coffee with someone you don't know.

Take a look at this example, then make your own comfort zone on the next page.

INNER COMFORT ZONE
Staying at home, watching a movie on TV, spending time with family, reading.

OUTER COMFORT ZONE
Shopping, going to the Movies, seeing close friends, taking the kids to school.

OUT OF COMFORT ZONE
Speaking in public, seeing people I dislike, meeting new people.

EXTREME OUT OF COMFORT ZONE
Singing in public, arguing, shouting, doing videos on social media.

Inner comfort zone

Outer comfort zone

Out of comfort zone

Extreme out of comfort zone

START YOUR DAY
RIGHT.

How you begin your day can set the tone for how the rest of your day will pan out. However, there are certain things we can do to help give us the best start.

1. A moment of calm. Before you get up, try a breathing exercise.
2. Make your bed as soon as you get up. Coming back into a tidy bedroom after your shower or breakfast will lift your spirits.
3. Make a to do list. List everything you need or want to achieve.

Use the space below to fill in your own mini-morning routine. Try to be realistic and not put too much pressure on yourself.

There are always flowers for those who wish to see them.

CO$_2$ Balance

This little technique is perfect for those times when you feel your anxiety may escalate into a panic attack. It helps to rebalance the CO2 in your system.

1. Cup your hands over your mouth and close your eyes.

2. Breathe in and out through your mouth as you would normally.

3. Continue breathing for one minute, or until you start to feel calm.

Tip: This technique can also work with a paper bag instead of using your hands.

REFLECTIONS MEDITATION

IF YOU HAVE QUESTIONS THAT KEEP
RATTLING AROUND YOUR HEAD, TRY THIS
MEDITATION TO SEE IF YOU CAN FIND THE
ANSWER. IF NOT, YOU MAY FIND PEACE
WITH NOT KNOWING.

1. Before you begin your meditation, write down the question or questions you would like the answers to. Don't type them or use your phone; get a pen and paper and write them down.

2. Sit in a comfortable position. As with the Basic Meditation, close your eyes and take a deep breath in through your nose and out through your mouth.

3. Listen to your breath and feel where your body makes contact with the ground, the chair, or the bed you are on.

4. After a few breaths, imagine the written question in your mind. Let the paper float before your closed eyes.

5. Think about the question as you breathe in, and blow out. Imagine the person you want to ask the question to. If the question is to yourself, imagine you are a stranger asking the question to you.

6. What answers do they give? If the answers make you sad, acknowledge this on the inhale, and blow away on the exhale.

7. If the questions are making you uneasy, let the paper float away until you can't see it anymore. Return to your breath.

8. Once you have answered or dismissed your questions, return to your breath. Listen to it and nothing else.

9. Slowly open your eyes.

TIP: IF YOUR QUESTIONS MAKE YOU UNCOMFORTABLE OR ANGRY, MAKE SURE YOU RELEASE THEM BEFORE YOU FINISH YOUR MEDITATION.

PEOPLE YOU ADMIRE

WHEN WE LOOK TO OTHERS FOR INSPIRATION, IT CAN OFTEN MAKE US FEEL HOPEFUL AND HAPPY. FILL IN THESE QUESTIONS ABOUT PEOPLE YOU ADMIRE AND WHY.

Which friend inspires you the most? ....

Why? ....

Which member of your family do you admire the most? ....

Why? ....

Which celebrity do you admire the most? ....

Why? ....

Which person on social media always makes you smile? ....

Why? ....

Which person at your work do you find the most inspiring? ....

Why? ....

USE THIS PAGE TO WRITE A LETTER TO ONE OF THESE PEOPLE. TELL THEM HOW MUCH YOU ADMIRE THEM AND WHY, AND THE EFFECT THEY HAVE HAD ON YOUR LIFE.

Be gentle on yourself,
it's tough out there.

MANTRA
MEDITATION

The act of repeating a saying or word over and over can help to go deeper into your meditation and promote positive thoughts.

1. Before you begin, think about what your mantra should be. It could be something you wish for yourself, or something you are trying to achieve. A single word mantra could be 'Peace,' 'Calm,' or 'Love,' or it could be a saying, such as 'I am strong enough,' 'I am loved,' etc.

2. Sit in a comfortable position. As with the Basic Meditation, close your eyes and take a deep breath in through your nose and out through your mouth.

3. Listen to your breath and feel where your body makes contact with the ground, the chair, or the bed you are on.

4. After at least six breaths, start to say your mantra on your exhale.

5. You can repeat your mantra as many times as you wish. Keep repeating for at least 30 minutes to go deep into your meditation.

6. Take at least three breaths in and out at the end of your meditation, then slowly open your eyes.

Tip: You can change your mantra each time you perform this meditation.

MUSIC AS MEDICINE

It has been proven that listening to music can calm the symptoms of anxiety. Whether it is an album of waves crashing on the beach, or a compilation of your favorite tracks, music can produce endorphins and give us the serotonin boost we all need now and then.

MY FAVORITE SONG:

THE SONG THAT MAKES ME WANT TO DANCE:

THE SONG THAT MAKES ME CRY WITH HAPPINESS:

THE SONG THAT REMINDS ME OF A HAPPY DAY:

THE SONG THAT REMINDS ME OF A SPECIAL PERSON:

DREAMS

Daydreaming isn't just for children. Visualizing something you really want and how you would act if you got it can calm the mind and help you focus on what you want to achieve.

USE THIS SPACE TO WRITE ABOUT YOUR HOPES AND DREAMS.

MY DREAM HOUSE WOULD BE:

IF I COULD LIVE ANYWHERE, I WOULD LIVE IN:

MY DREAM JOB WOULD BE TO:

MY DREAM RELATIONSHIP WOULD BE:

THE DREAMS I HAVE FOR MY FAMILY ARE:

OF ALL THESE THINGS, THE MOST IMPORTANT TO ME IS:

FEELING YOUR BREATH WORK

This exercise will show you how you physically use your breath, which will help you with lots of the other exercises in this book.

1. Lie on your back on the floor. You can use a cushion to support your head.

2. Take a deep breath in through your nose and out through your mouth.

3. Place your hand on the part of your chest / stomach that rises the most.

4. If your hand ended up on the top part of your chest, you're not using the whole of your lungs.

5. This time, try and make your stomach inflate like a balloon.

6. Continue taking breaths in and out and notice where your torso rises. Try to make your stomach and diaphragm the highest points.

Tip: This is a good thing to remember during most of the exercises in this book. Try and breathe into your stomach.

"Close down all the unnecessary tabs on your mind's computer."

SOUND MEDITATION

If you find it hard to get into a meditative state, or if you are somewhere with a lot of background noise, this could be the practice for you.

1. Find a noise you are comfortable listening to. It must be something continuous that will fill your mind. It could be whale calls, waves, or white noise. There are lots of playlists on streaming services you can search to find the one for you.

2. Ideally, put on a pair of headphones. If you don't, make sure you are in a room where you won't be disturbed and can turn the volume as high as it needs to be to drown out other sounds. Perhaps set a timer for this one.

3. Sit in a comfortable position. You can lie down or sit down as you feel best.

4. As with the Basic Meditation, close your eyes and take a deep breath in through your nose and out through your mouth.

5. Pay attention to your breath and feel where your body makes contact with the ground, the chair, or the bed you are on.

6. Feel where your body rests or connects with other parts of your body. Feel the weight and the heat.

7. As you inhale and exhale, try to forget any other sensory experience. If you feel too cold, acknowledge it and know that it won't be for long. The same goes if your stomach rumbles!

8. Focus on your breath and your body. When you hear your timer, open your eyes and slowly start to connect to your body.

Tip: Take your time when selecting your sound. You want to choose something you are going to be comfortable listening to.

YOU ARE AWESOME

Sometimes we all need reminding about how great we really are. We all do something well, whether it's writing music or cooking grilled sandwiches. Use this space to record what you do well.

The best thing I cook is: ....

I like what I wear because: ....

I am a good friend because: ....

My family members like me being
around because: ....

The best thing I can draw is: ....

I am really good at: ....

I am really supportive of: ....

I really care about: ....

THE LONGER EXHALE

This simple trick is one to remember if you don't have time to get into a long exercise.

1. Breathe in through your nose for 4 counts.

2. Pause, then exhale slowly through your mouth for 8 counts.

3. Breathe out more than you would on a normal breath, imagining your whole body emptying.

4. Repeat at least three times.

Tip: This exercise can be done discreetly, so it is great for times when you can't leave your desk, or that awkward social gathering!

"Take time each day to count your blessings."

Tidy Home, Tidy Mind

You don't have to do a full Marie Kondo to your home to make you feel better, but tackling those trifling DIY jobs can give you the lift you might need.

Walk around your house, or even the room you are now in and make a list of what you need to do to make it tidier, and what you would like to do. It could be anything from cleaning out a drawer to re-hanging the curtains. Seeing these jobs each day without doing them is like a knock with a tiny hammer. Think how proud of yourself you will be once they are done.

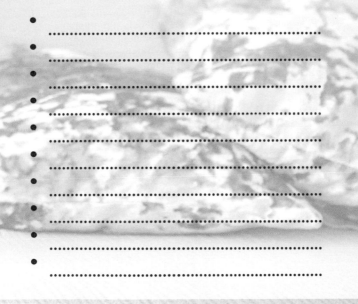

- ....
- ....
- ....
- ....
- ....
- ....
- ....
- ....
- ....
- ....

DRAW YOUR BREATH

This meditation is great for people who like to visualize and have a creative side. Grab your journal or a piece of paper and get started.

1. Find the materials you would like to use. This could be a pencil, pen, or marker. Try and pick something free flowing that doesn't need you to press too hard.

2. Sit in a comfortable position with your materials close at hand. As with the Basic Meditation, take a deep breath in through your nose and out through your mouth.

3. Listen to your breath and feel where your body makes contact with the ground, the chair, or the bed you are on.

4. Pay attention to how your pen sits in your hand. Inhale, and as you exhale, draw a straight line. Concentrate on how that feels and how the ink sinks into the paper.

5. Now, draw as you inhale and draw as you exhale. Some people draw this as a wavy line, others as wiggles and straight lines. Do what feels natural.

6. As you come to the end of your paper, or as many pages of your journal as you want to use, rest your hand on the table.

7. Close your eyes and take three more breaths to finish.

Tip: As tempting as it might be to use paints, this requires stopping to dip your brush into the paint, and would therefore disrupt the flow.

STOMACH BREATHING

This exercise really engages your stomach muscles and draws your focus to your body.

1. Lie down in a comfortable position. On the floor is perfect, but if this is uncomfortable, your bed or couch will work just as well.

2. Breathe in through your nose, making your stomach rise. Try to keep your chest as flat as possible.

3. When you feel as though you can't take in any more air comfortably, exhale through your mouth as though you are blowing out a candle.

4. Again, ensure it is your stomach that is falling and emptying of air.

5. Think about your stomach muscles each time you breathe in and out.

6. Repeat at least three times, or more if you have time.

TIP: TAKE TIME WITH YOUR BREATH; IT TAKES PRACTICE TO GET THIS EXERCISE RIGHT.

YOU ARE THE GREATEST

What does your mind think about in the early hours of the morning? Does it remember that time you gave an amazing presentation at work, or the time you forgot your friend's birthday? For most people, it is the latter. Our failures seem to burn themselves into our memories, while we often forget the times we were, quite frankly, brilliant.

Use the space below to list five times you were great.

1.
2.
3.
4.
5.

JUST LIKE
THE MOON, YOU
ARE YOU –

NO MATTER
WHAT PHASE
YOU ARE GOING
THROUGH.

This meditation is for those times when you feel there is too much negativity in the world, or someone you feel needs extra positivity sent their way.

1. Think about what you want to achieve with this meditation. Do you want to cancel out negative thoughts? Clear the air of negativity? Or perhaps send love to someone in particular?

2. Sit in a comfortable position. As with the Basic Meditation, close your eyes and take a deep breath in through your nose and out through your mouth.

3. Listen to your breath and feel where your body makes contact with the ground, the chair, or the bed you are on.

4. On your inhale, think about what you want to achieve. Think about the person, the message, the positivity, and the love.

5. On the exhalation, imagine you are blowing that message, that love, wherever it needs to go.

6. Keep repeating your message until you feel you have done as much as you want or can.

7. Finish your meditation by thinking of all the things you can do to love and take care of yourself.

Tip: This meditation is the perfect antidote to the negativity that can spread on social media. It brings you back to a center of positivity.

WARM
FACE
TECHNIQUE

This exercise will make you feel comforted in times of high anxiety.

1. Sit or stand comfortably.

2. Rub the palms of your hands together quickly, as though you have a piece of wood to start a fire.

3. Place your hands over your eyes, with your palms on either side of your nose.

4. Breathe in deeply for 4 counts through your nose and out for 4 counts through your mouth.

5. Repeat three times, or until you start to feel soothed.

Tip: Use this technique when you feel unhappy and are in need of some comfort.

"It will all work out in the end, and if it hasn't worked out, it is not the end."

Fist and release

This technique is perfect for times of extreme tension and anxiety.

1. Stand with your feet hip-width apart and your arms at your side.

2. As you breathe in, squeeze your hands into tight fists. Try to visualize all of your tension being balled up into your hands.

3. Blow out your breath quickly through your mouth. At the same time, release your fists, spreading your fingers out wide.

4. Try to visualize your tension running through your fingers and out through your fingertips.

5. Repeat at least twice, or as many times as you need.

Tip: Remember to keep your arms straight throughout the exercise.

YOU ARE BIGGER THAN WHATEVER MAKES YOU ANXIOUS.

OH, HAPPY DAY!

When you are having a bad day, it's always a good idea to focus on happier times. Take a moment or two to write a diary entry about one of your happiest days.

It doesn't have to be momentous (such as a wedding), it could be a lazy Sunday where you picnicked in the backyard. Remember your happy times and let this give you strength before carrying on with your day.

The Small Things

There is joy to be found in the simplest of moments. Take time to think about your day (if you are reading this at night) or yesterday (if you are reading this in the daytime).

The moment that made me happiest was...

Something that made me laugh was...

The most beautiful thing I saw was...

I felt most at ease when...

I was proud when...

You will only be happy when you let go of things you cannot control.

Five Things

When life gets overwhelming, your anxiety can threaten to take over. Perform this meditation when life feels a little too much.

1. Stand with your legs hip-width apart and start to focus on your breath.

2. Breathe in through your mouth and out through your nose.

3. Keep your eyes open and register five things you can see. It could be the sky, the grass, your carpet, your bed, etc.

4. Now think of five things you can feel. It could be the wind on your face, wool against your skin, or your hands against your legs.

5. Now register five things you can hear. It could be a lawnmower, someone typing, or a bird singing.

6. Keep up your breath and you should start to feel calmer. Repeat the cycle, trying to find new things if you feel it would benefit.

Tip: This meditation can be performed without anyone knowing you are meditating. It is a great way to calm an anxious mind and bring you back to your center.

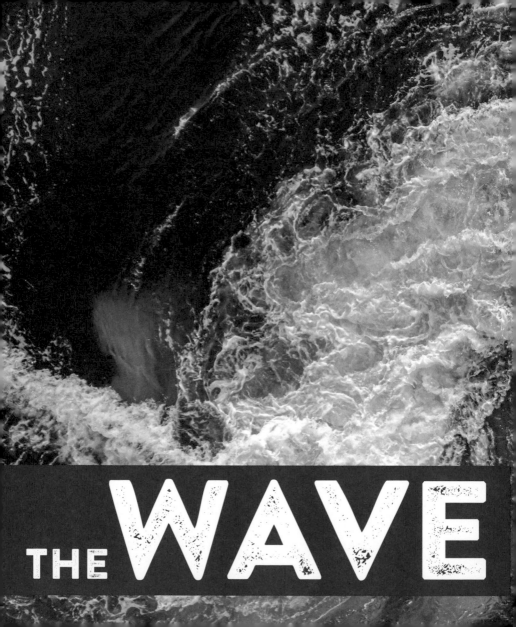

THE WAVE

THIS IS THE PERFECT EXERCISE TO DO AT THE BEACH, OR FOR THOSE WHO WISH THEY WERE!

1. STAND, SIT, OR LIE DOWN IN A COMFORTABLE POSITION.

2. CLOSE YOUR EYES AND INHALE FOR 3 COUNTS. AS YOU DO, IMAGINE A WAVE DRAWING BACK AWAY FROM THE SHORE.

3. PAUSE FOR 1 COUNT, THEN BLOW AWAY YOUR BREATH FOR 3 COUNTS. IMAGINE THAT THIS IS THE WAVE CRASHING BACK ONTO THE BEACH.

4. ADAPT YOUR WAVE TO SUIT HOW YOU FEEL. IF YOU ARE FEELING VERY STRESSED OR ANXIOUS, MAKE THE WAVE HIGH AND DRAMATIC. WITH EACH NEW BREATH / WAVE, MAKE THE EXHALING WAVE LESS DRAMATIC UNTIL IT IS A GENTLE ROLL.

5. CONTINUE FOR AS LONG AS YOU FEEL IS NECESSARY.

TIP: IF YOU ARE AT THE BEACH, MATCH YOUR BREATH TO THE WAVES THAT YOU HEAR. YOU COULD USE A BEACH SOUNDTRACK IF IT HELPS YOU TO VISUALIZE.

Who Am I?

This is an ancient form of meditation that helps to focus the mind on the self.

1. Sit or lie down in a comfortable position.

2. As with the Basic Meditation, close your eyes and take a deep breath in through your nose and out through your mouth.

3. Listen to your breath and feel where your body makes contact with the ground, the chair, or the bed you are on.

4. As you breathe, ask the following questions. Who am I? What do I love? What makes me who I am?

5. Your brain will naturally want to answer with words; your name, the names of people you love, etc, but you must try and ignore them.

6. Each time a thought comes into your mind that isn't the question or your breath, you must quietly dismiss it.

7. Repeat the questions until you can say them without immediately trying to answer them.

8. Give yourself a long inhalation in and out before opening your eyes.

Tip: This meditation can take time to perfect, so don't worry if you don't get it right first time.

IT IS OKAY TO FEEL BRAVE AND SCARED AT THE SAME TIME.

The List

Without thinking too hard, list all
the things you would miss the most
if they were no longer in your life.
They could be people or possessions.

Start Planning

Getting your mind out of the present and into the future can be the perfect way to quiet anxiety. By planning day trips, work tasks, or projects at home, your brain automatically feels more organized and able to cope.

Use the following page to plan five things you would like to do or need to do this year.

This ancient technique will help to rid your stomach of anxiety.

LION'S

1. Get into a comfortable kneeling position. You can use a cushion on the floor if it helps you.

2. Cross your ankles over each other and sit back on them. If this isn't comfortable, try sitting cross-legged.

3. Place your hands on your thighs and take a deep breath in.

4. As you breathe out, open your mouth wide and breathe out the word 'Ha!' as though you are roaring like a lion.

5. Relax your face as you breathe in once more.

6. Repeat at least three times.

Word
Breathing

Focusing on a single word will help your breath to come more naturally.

1. Concentrate on how you are feeling. What word comes to mind when you think of how you want to feel? It could be 'safe,' 'calm,' 'loved,' etc.

2. Breathe in slowly for 4 counts.

3. Exhale for 4 counts. As you exhale, imagine your word clearly in your mind. Repeat it over and over.

4. On your second breath in, imagine you are taking in all of your anxiety. As you breathe out, repeat your word again, drowning out any negativity.

Tip: Think about your word before you start your inhale. If it helps you to think more visually, imagine the word in a bright lightbulb or neon lettering.

"Kindness is free; give as much of it away as you can."

Spider Map

This quick exercise can be repeated anytime you have episodes of anxiety and have a scrap piece of paper nearby.

Start by writing your name in the center of the page. Now, draw lines and bubbles to all the worrying things that are triggering your anxiety. Off each of those bubbles, write how you can help or counteract those worries. Try here:

THE CORK BOARD

1. Sit or lie down in a comfortable position. Ensure that you won't be disturbed for the next 20-30 minutes.

2. As with the Basic Meditation, close your eyes and take a deep breath in through your nose and out through your mouth.

3. Listen to your breath and feel where your body makes contact with the ground, the chair, or the bed you are on.

4. Now, think of all the things that might be worrying you at the moment. As you think of them, imagine they are being written on pieces of paper and placed in front of you.

5. Now think of all the things that you are grateful for. Again, they should appear on pieces of paper.

6. In your mind's eye, imagine a large cork board in front of you.

7. Take all the most important things from the table in front of you and put them on the cork board. You can only take five.

8. If a stress or a worry is on your cork board, that is okay. However, you should try and have at least three things you are grateful for so that the good outweighs the bad. You can rearrange them as much as you like.

9. Think about these five things as you inhale and exhale. As you exhale, imagine your breath drying out the ink on the negative thoughts.

10. As you open your eyes, you should start to see more clearly what matters and what does not.

Top tip: When you repeat this meditation, try to note how some of the things you found stressful or negative the last time no longer make it onto the table.

Comparison is the thief of joy.

"
Don't let painful moments define you. Let them make you stronger, braver, and kinder.
"

EMERGENCY TOOLKIT!

All you need to do to create your toolkit is to think of things that calm your own feelings of anxiety.

Gather the physical things you need and put them in a spare box or bag. Place it somewhere you'll know where to find it, such as under your bed or in a cabinet.

Your kit could include pictures of your loved ones, a smell you love, a little treat that makes you feel better, a book of affirmations, a mindful coloring book, etc. Anything that makes you feel lighter.

What will be in your kit?

Buzzing
Bee Breath

THIS YOGA-CENTRIC TECHNIQUE IS GOOD FOR
THOSE WHO HOLD TENSION IN THEIR FOREHEADS.

1. SIT COMFORTABLY. THIS COULD BE
CROSS-LEGGED OR ON A CHAIR.

2. PLACE YOUR INDEX FINGERS ON THE TRAGUS
CARTILAGE (THE SMALL PIECE OF CARTILAGE THAT
PARTLY COVERS THE EAR).

3. TAKE A BREATH IN THROUGH YOUR
NOSE FOR 4 COUNTS.

4. AS YOU BREATHE OUT THROUGH YOUR NOSE,
PRESS THE TRAGUS CARTILAGE TO COVER YOUR EAR.
KEEP YOUR MOUTH CLOSED AND HUM. THE NOISE
SHOULD FILL YOUR HEAD.

5. REPEAT AS MANY TIMES AS YOU LIKE.

TIP: KEEP HUMMING FOR AS LONG
AS IT TAKES FOR THE BREATH TO
LEAVE YOUR BODY.

A glitch on your phone can often be fixed by switching it off for a while. The same applies to you.

Positivity Jar

This little jar can sit on your desk or your kitchen counter. Reach for it when you need a positive boost.

What to do:
- Find a clean, empty jar with a lid.

- Each time you hear or read an affirmation that you like, write it down, fold it up, and pop it in the jar.

- You can decorate the jar or leave it as it is. Pull out an affirmation when you are feeling low.

YOUR HAPPY PLACE

Anxiety can lead our minds into a dark corner, and it can feel hard to escape. You can use this practice to lead your thoughts out into the light.

Use the space on the right to write down your thoughts or use this as a visualization technique. It is particularly useful when late night anxiety is preventing you from sleep.

- Imagine your 'happy place.' Your happy place can be a real place, or somewhere imaginary. It can be anywhere in the world, from a tropical beach to your own living room.

- Start by thinking of the atmosphere. Is it warm? Cold? Are you inside or outside? Is it day or night?

- Now start to populate your surroundings. If you are inside, what furniture is there? What is on the floor and walls? If you are outside, what can you see? Is there sand, trees, or are you somewhere urban?

- Add as much detail as you can. Only add things that make you happy. If you love a room in your house, but hate the wallpaper, change it. If you love walking in the woods, but don't like mushrooms, get rid of them.

- When your space is perfect, add people or animals if you want them. If not, that's fine too.

Happiness Journal

Happiness is everywhere, if we only look hard enough.
Use this space to record the good things that have
happened to you this week.

A nice thing I saw or read in the news was:

Something delicious I ate was:

A person / animal I really enjoyed
spending time with was:

A great moment at work was:

A plan I have made that makes me happy is:

A nice thing someone said was:

NOTES